You will keep in perfect peace all who trust in you, all whose thoughts are fixed on you!

Isaiah 26:3

Give all your worries and cares to God, for he cares about you.

1 Peter 5:7

Then Jesus said, "Come to me, all of you who are weary and carry heavy burdens, and I will give you rest.

Matthew 11:28

For I can do everything through Christ,
who gives me strength.

Philippians 4:13

The name of the LORD is a strong fortress; the godly run to him and are safe.

A friend is always loyal, and a brother is born to help in time of need.

Proverbs 17:17

There is no greater love than to lay down one's life for one's friends.

Be on guard. Stand firm in the faith. Be courageous. Be strong.

1 Corinthians 16:13

Look to the LORD and his strength; seek his face always.

The LORD is my shepherd; I have all that
I need.

Psalm 23:1

For God has not given us a spirit of fear and timidity, but of power, love, and self-discipline.

He gives power to the weak and strength to the powerless.

God is our refuge and strength, always
ready to help in times of trouble.

Psalm 46:1

People who conceal their sins will not prosper, but if they confess and turn from them, they will receive mercy

Proverbs 28:13

Then he says, "I will never again remember their sins and lawless deeds."

Hebrews 10:17

He has removed our sins as far from us as
the east is from the west.

"Don't let your hearts be troubled. Trust in God, and trust also in me.

John 14:1

Trust in the LORD with all your heart; do not depend on your own understanding.

Proverbs 3:5

But when I am afraid, I will put my trust in you.

Worry weighs a person down; an encouraging word cheers a person up.

Proverbs 12:25

Be happy with those who are happy, and weep with those who weep.

Romans 12:15

God blesses those who mourn, for they will be comforted.

Now let your unfailing love comfort me,
just as you promised me, your servant.

Psalm 119:76

For no one is abandoned by the Lord forever.

Lamentations 3:31

The LORD himself will fight for you. Just stay calm.

Exodus 14:14

So humble yourselves before God. Resist the devil, and he will flee from you.

James 4:7

Trust in the LORD with all your heart; do not depend on your own understanding.

Proverbs 3:5

So if the Son sets you free, you are truly free.

John 8:36

O Lord, you are so good, so ready to forgive, so full of unfailing love for all who ask for your help.

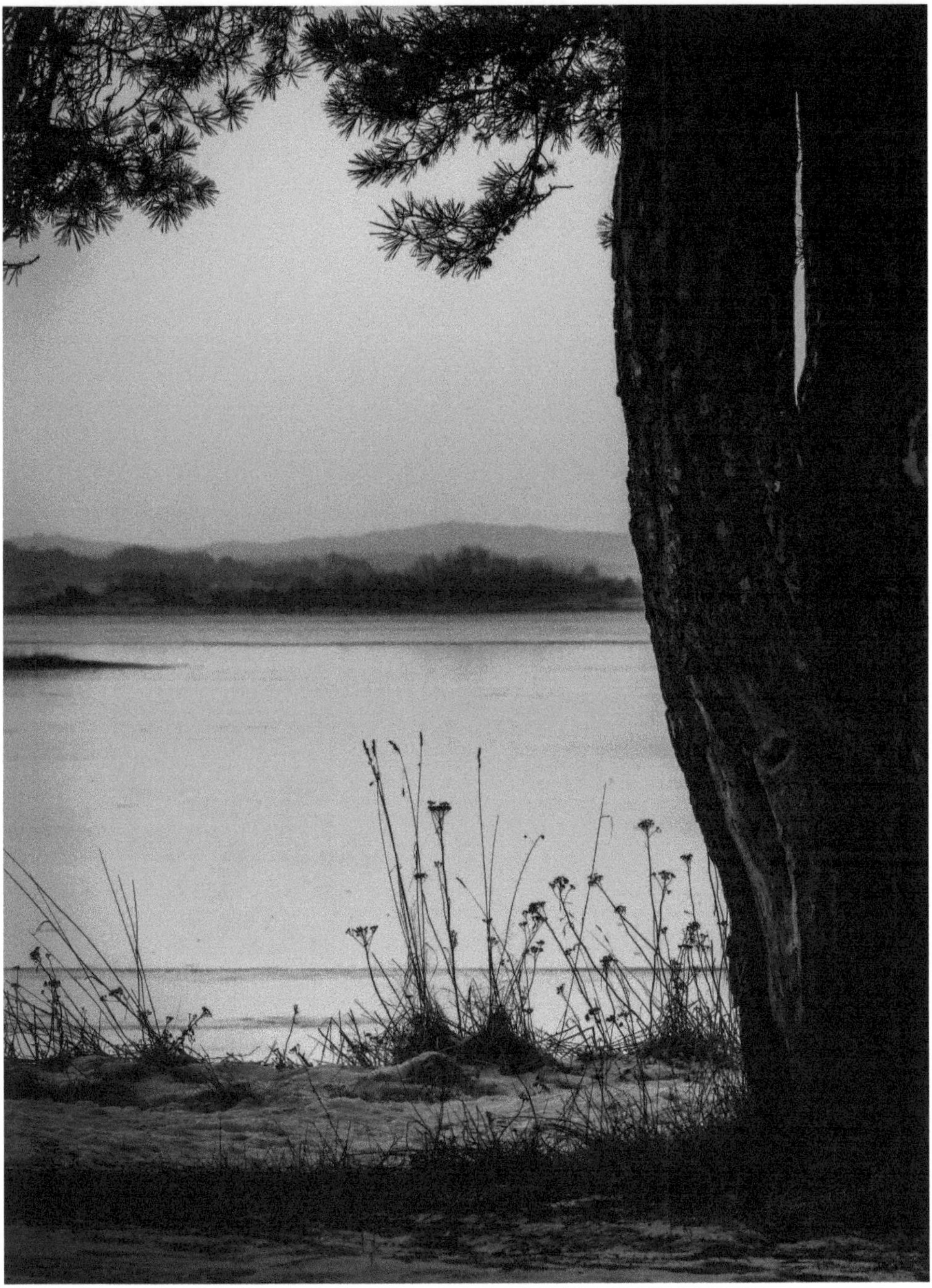

"You parents—if your children ask for a loaf of bread, do you give them a stone instead?"

Matthew 7:9

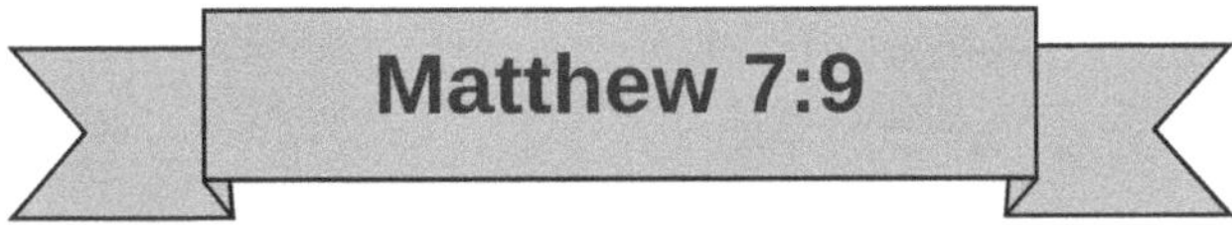

What shall we say about such wonderful things as these? If God is for us, who can ever be against us?

Romans 8:31

Direct your children onto the right path, and when they are older, they will not leave it.

Proverbs 22:6

So faith comes from hearing, that is,
hearing the Good News about Christ.

Romans 10:17

Faith shows the reality of what we hope for;
it is the evidence of things we cannot see.

So encourage each other and build each other up, just as you are already doing.

Thessalonians 5:11

Rejoice in our confident hope. Be patient in trouble, and keep on praying.

Romans 12:12

O Lord, if you heal me, I will be truly healed;
if you save me, I will be truly saved.

Jeremiah 17:14

I will give you back your health
and heal your wounds," says the Lord.

Dear friend, I hope all is well with you and that you are as healthy in body as you are strong in spirit.

3 John 1:2

Have compassion on me, Lord, for I am weak.
Heal me, Lord, for my bones are in agony.

Psalms 6:2

We love each other because he loved us first.

1 John 4:19

Hatred stirs up quarrels, but love makes
up for all offenses.

Proverbs 10:12

But God showed his great love for us by sending
Christ to die for us while we were still sinners.

Romans 5:8

Three things will last forever—faith, hope, and love—and the greatest of these is love.

1 Corinthians 13:13

Most important of all, continue to show deep love for each other, for love covers a multitude of sins.

1 Peter 4:8

Above all, clothe yourselves with love, which
binds us all together in perfect harmony.

Colossians 3:14

And do everything with love.

1 Corinthians 16:14

The man who finds a wife finds a treasure,
and he receives favor from the Lord.

Proverbs 18:22

Get rid of all bitterness, rage, anger, harsh words, and slander, as well as all types of evil behavior.

Love prospers when a fault is forgiven, but dwelling on it separates close friends.

Proverbs 17:9

The LORD directs the steps of the godly. He delights in every detail of their lives.

Psalm 37:23

Now repent of your sins and turn to God,
so that your sins may be wiped away.

Then he says, "I will never again remember their sins and lawless deeds."

Hebrews 10:17

For everything there is a season, a time
for every activity under heaven.

Ecclesiastes 3:1

But the Lord our God is merciful and forgiving,
even though we have rebelled against him.

Daniel 9:9

Pray like this: Our Father in heaven, may your name be kept holy.

Matthew 6:9

Your promise revives me; it comforts me
in all my troubles.

Be on guard. Stand firm in the faith. Be courageous. Be strong.

1 Corinthians 16:13

The faithful love of the LORD never ends!
His mercies never cease.

Lamentations 3:22

For he will rescue you from every trap and protect you from deadly disease.